B U S T A R D

LEGENDS & LEAGUES

W O R K B O O K

www.VeritasPress.com
(800) 922-5082

First Edition 2004

Copyright ©2004 Veritas Press
www.VeritasPress.com
ISBN 978-1-932168-24-2

Printed in the United States of America.

LEGENDS & LEAGUES

Table of CONTENTS

After reading the book *Legends & Leagues, or How Mr. Tardy Gets from Here to There,* complete this workbook. Each project is linked to the book with page numbers (in the upper right hand corner) to aid the teacher in explaining the concepts. This program can be used as a unit study or stretched out over a year, doing one project a week while singing the song as part of your regular Memory Time. We also recommend using Audio Memory's *Geography Songs* and *States & Capitals* to memorize the states and countries.

MAKE PAPER DOLLS 5

MAKING A STRIP MAP 6

ICONS OR SYMBOLS 7

MAKE A MAP 8

MAKE A COMPASS 11

POLAR BEARS & PENGUINS 12

SUNRISE SUNSET 13

ZOOLOGICAL GRID 14

PARALLELS AND MERIDIANS 15

PARALLELS OF THE CLASSROOM 16

TARDY'S PUZZLE 17

MR. LATITUDE'S EQUATOR 18

COLOR THE CONTINENTS 19

ANIMALS AND CONTINENTS 20

CUT AND PASTE GEOGRAPHY 25

MATCHING GEOGRAPHY 26

DRAW STATE LANDMARKS 27

COLOR MAGELLAN 35

TIME ZONES 36

COLOR THE EARTH 37

TREASURE HUNT 38

FEET & SCALE 39

FINAL EXAM 40

MEMORY SONG 42

A SHORT GLOSSARY 44

LEGENDS & LEAGUES

*"Allow me to introduce myself—I am Mr. Longitude,
and my wide friend here is Mr. Latitude."*

Photocopy this page onto card stock then color
the figures. Cut along the dotted lines, then glue
Mr. Longitude to the cardboard tube from a
roll of paper towels. Glue Mr. Latitude
to the cardboard tube from a roll
of toilet paper.

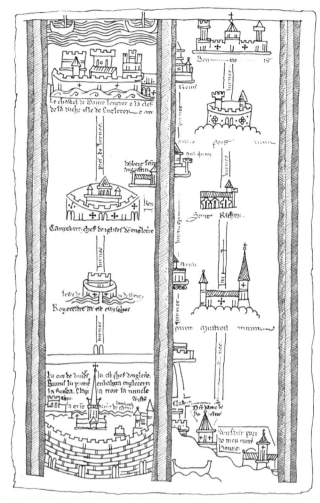

If you look carefully on the walls of the office where the story occurs, you will find a 13th-century strip map that shows the way from London to Dover Castle, and over the English Channel to some towns in France.

Strip maps have been used for a very long time. They were used in ancient Egypt; the Romans used them; and the Chinese used strip maps made on silk. In 1259 A.D. a monk drew up the Chronica Majora, a strip map that showed the way from his home in London to Jerusalem. Nowadays, automobile associations and websites make custom strip maps for modern day travellers.

In this project we will make a strip map because it is a very basic map. Have the students draw pictures of their homes, their grandparents' homes and things they see on their way to visit their grandparents. Cut these out and glue them onto a piece of paper laid out vertically in the order that they are encountered. Begin at the bottom and end with the grandparent's house at the top of the page—as shown in the example below.

LEGENDS &LEAGUES

"Maps are useful things that have the big things around us drawn in small, simple pictures."

A map is a picture to help you get from Here to There. Below are small pictures that are made to make you think of the real thing that they represent. They are called symbols and can be found on maps, signs and other places where people need direction. Draw a line from the symbol to the word it represents.

✈	hospital	stairway	?
🚢	airport	school	🚆
🚻	no parking	barbershop	⚑
🍴	marina	trash	🗑
☎	handicap access	church	✂
♿	restrooms	information	stairs
®	telephone	elevator	elevator
✚	food	subway	⛪

"There are big maps and little maps, flat maps and round maps. There are city maps and country maps, maps with words and maps with symbols. And there have even been woven and carved maps."

Review the maps on this page and the next, then make a similar map of your classroom or bedroom on another piece of paper or the space provided on page 10. This map you make will be looking at the room as you never have before, from the point of view of a fly walking on the ceiling. After making the map, think of other maps you can make (of your school desk,

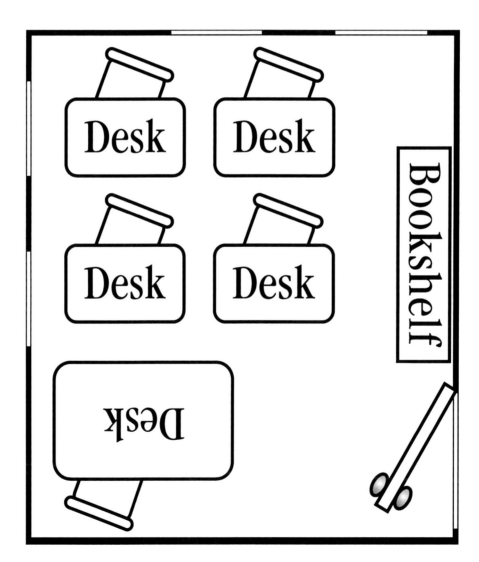

home, block, local grocery store, etc.) and what materials you can use to make the map (Wikki Stix™, pipe cleaners, construction paper, straws, etc.). Remember that Mr. Latitude on page 12 held a woven map of sticks and shells like those that sailors made in the Marshall Islands in the Pacific Ocean over 500 years ago. These maps used sticks to show ocean currents and the shells attached to them represented the islands they were sailing to. On page 13 Mr. Longitude held a wooden map like the ones that the people of Greenland and Canada carved of the coastlines to help them when hunting and fishing.

Another fun project for an entire class would be to make a map that shows where each student lives, then travel to each house on a field trip for snacks and games at each stop.

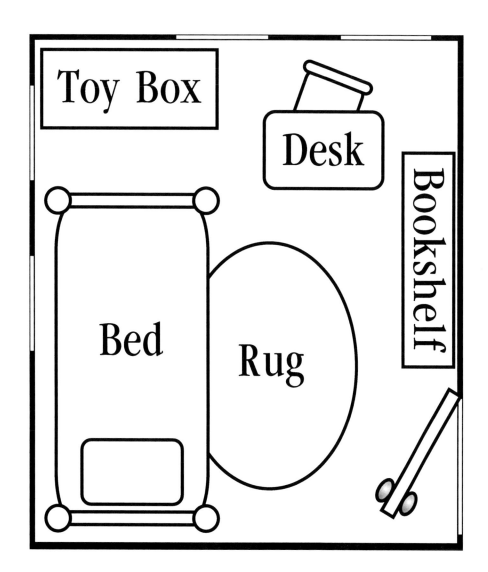

LEGENDS & LEAGUES

Make a
MAP
PAGE 12

LEGENDS & LEAGUES

"Most maps have something called a compass drawn on them that shows direction and has at least four points showing which way is North, South, East and West," instructed Mr. Latitude.

Stroke the eye of a needle across a magnet sixty times, going in the same direction each time. Place a small piece of paper on top of water. Set the needle on top of the paper and gently move the paper to cause it to spin slightly. Make sure there is no metal nearby and that the magnet used to magnetize the needle is away from the bowl. When the needle and paper have stopped moving, the sharp end of the needle will be pointing north.

Materials

1 sewing needle

1 magnet

1 bowl of water

1 small piece of paper

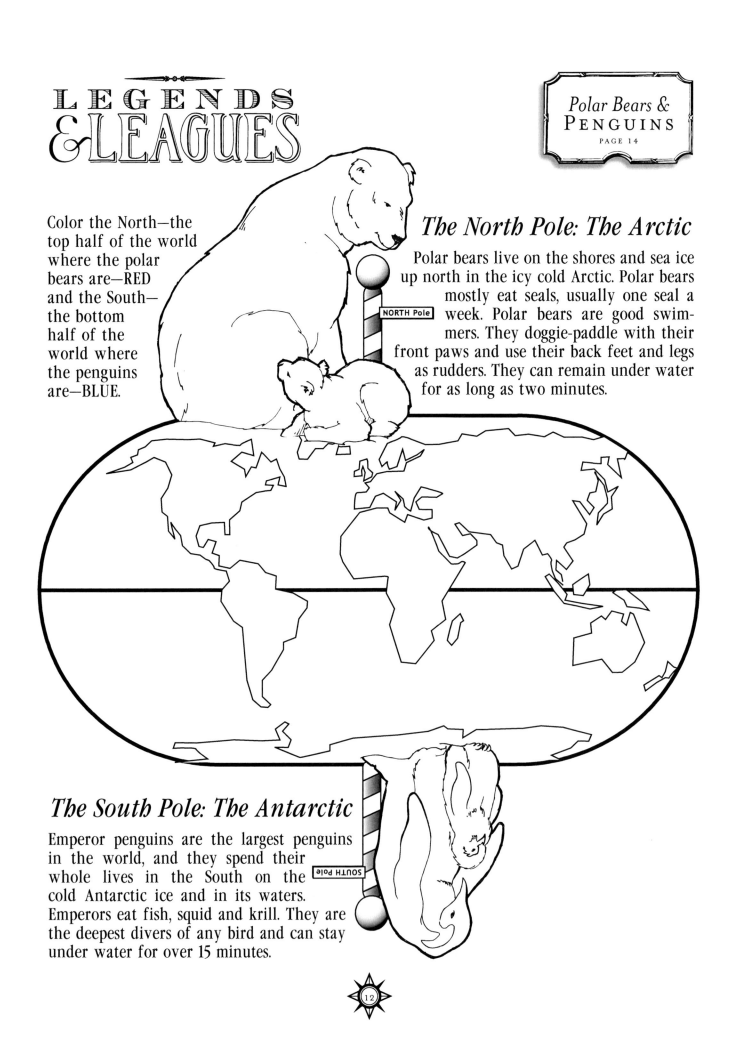

LEGENDS &LEAGUES

Color the North—the top half of the world where the polar bears are—RED and the South—the bottom half of the world where the penguins are—BLUE.

The North Pole: The Arctic

Polar bears live on the shores and sea ice up north in the icy cold Arctic. Polar bears mostly eat seals, usually one seal a week. Polar bears are good swimmers. They doggie-paddle with their front paws and use their back feet and legs as rudders. They can remain under water for as long as two minutes.

NORTH Pole

SOUTH Pole

The South Pole: The Antarctic

Emperor penguins are the largest penguins in the world, and they spend their whole lives in the South on the cold Antarctic ice and in its waters. Emperors eat fish, squid and krill. They are the deepest divers of any bird and can stay under water for over 15 minutes.

LEGENDS & LEAGUES

"East and West are the other points of the compass. East is where the Sun comes up in the morning, and West is where the Sun goes down every night," said Mr. Longitude.

Mr. Tardy is still confused about East and West. Color the Sun that is setting in the West red and the Sun that is rising in the East yellow.

Color the animal red that is one space directly south of the bear.
Color the animal blue that is one space directly west of the camel.
Color the animal yellow that is one space directly north of the walrus.
Color the animal green that is one space directly east of the elephant.

LEGENDS & LEAGUES

"Some of my favorite things on maps are the elegant lines that run around the world from East to West—called parallels."

Mr. Latitude likes the lines called parallels because they help you find your latitude on a map (your position up and down). Meridians are Mr. Longitude's favorites because they help locate your longitude (your position left to right). By using both latitude and longitude you can describe where you are or where you want to go without ever having been there or even knowing the name of the place. You can locate places on a map using a similar feature that uses letters and numbers from a grid. Label the cities on the map according to their dot's coordinates on the grid.

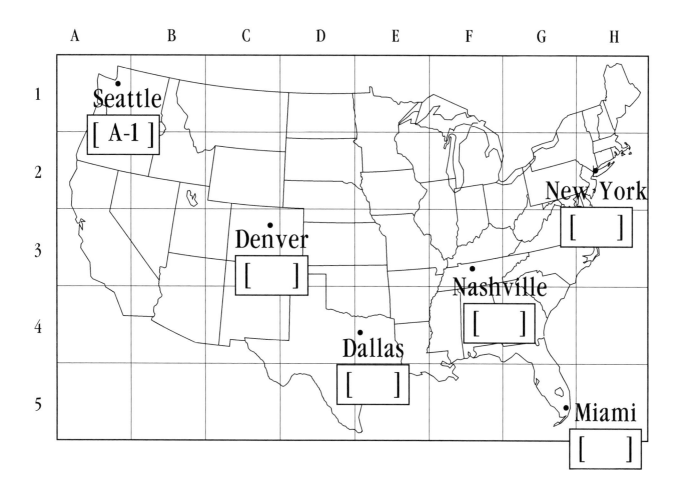

LEGENDS & LEAGUES

"Some of my favorite things on maps are the elegant lines that run around the world from East to West—called parallels."

Create a grid in your classroom (or bedroom) using lengths of yarn stretched on the floor as shown below. Make signs for A through D and 1 through 4 and place them at their appropriate positions. Announce a coordinate (e.g., B-3) and have the students take turns identifying what furniture or objects are located there. After doing several coordinates, instead announce an object (e.g., the trash can) and have a student give you the coordinate.

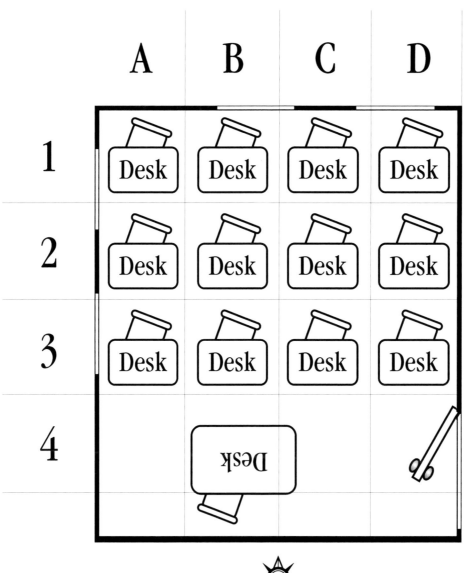

LEGENDS & LEAGUES

"I've never seen any lines like that when I've walked around outside," Mr. Tardy said with a puzzled look on his face.

Color the puzzle below then cut along the solid black lines to make a Mr. Tardy puzzle.

LEGENDS & LEAGUES

"The Equator runs around the middle of our world like the belt on my trousers—" Mr. Latitude illustrated, *"dividing the world into the Northern and Southern Hemispheres."*

Color Mr. Latitude then cut around the outside of the character, fold at the feet and glue together. When the glue has dried, fold along the dotted lines on his back so that he can "close" his jacket.

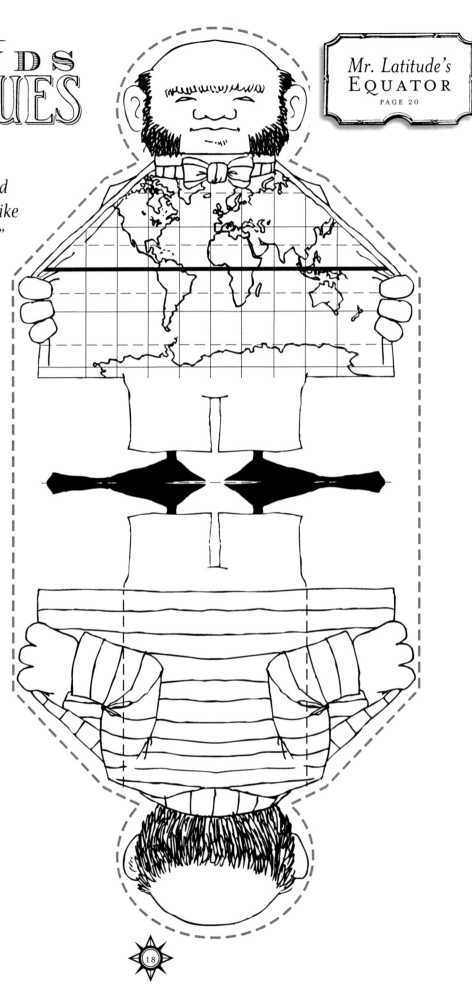

LEGENDS & LEAGUES

Color the
CONTINENTS
PAGE 22

"In between the world's four oceans are giant piles of land called Continents."

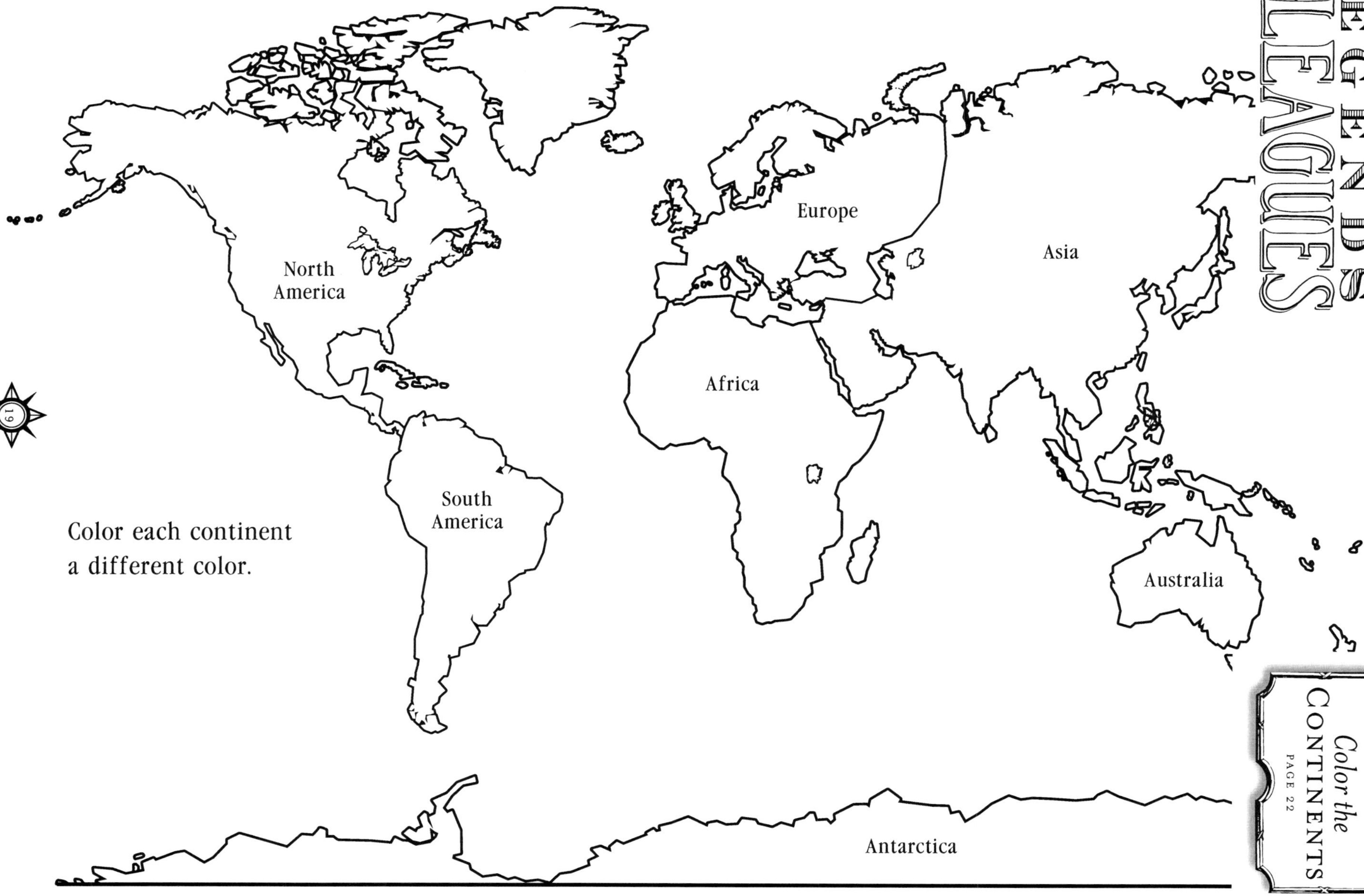

Australia

Asia

Europe

Africa

Antarctica

North
America

South
America

Color each continent
a different color.

19

LEGENDS & LEAGUES

The next four pages have a map to photocopy, cut out, and tape together (each page overlaps slightly). Label and color each continent to match page 19, then cut out the animals on this page and paste them on the continent they belong to by using the clues below each animal.

Glue the Armadillo
in North America

Glue the Bald Eagle
in North America

Glue the Bustard Bird
in Europe

Glue the Emperor
Penguin in Antarctica

Glue the Piranha
in South America

Glue the Platypus
in Australia

Glue the Snowy Owl
in Asia

Glue the Cobra
in Asia

Glue the Scorpion
in Africa

Glue the Polar Bear
in the North America

Glue the Tiger
in Asia

Glue the Okapi
in Africa

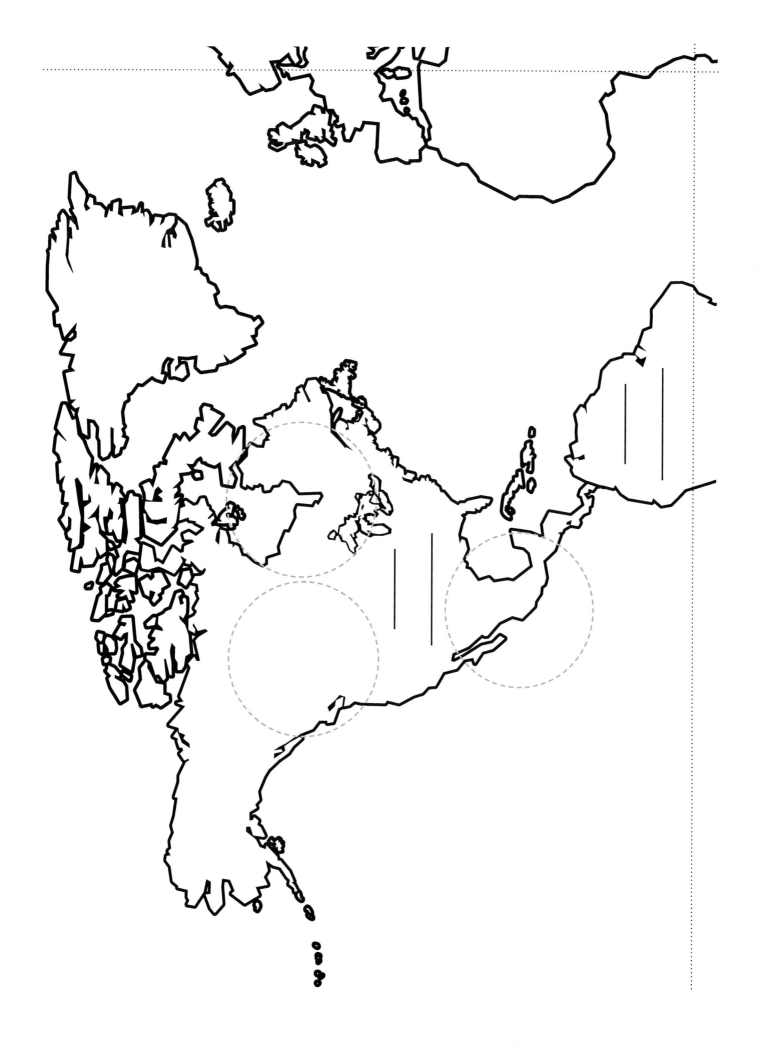

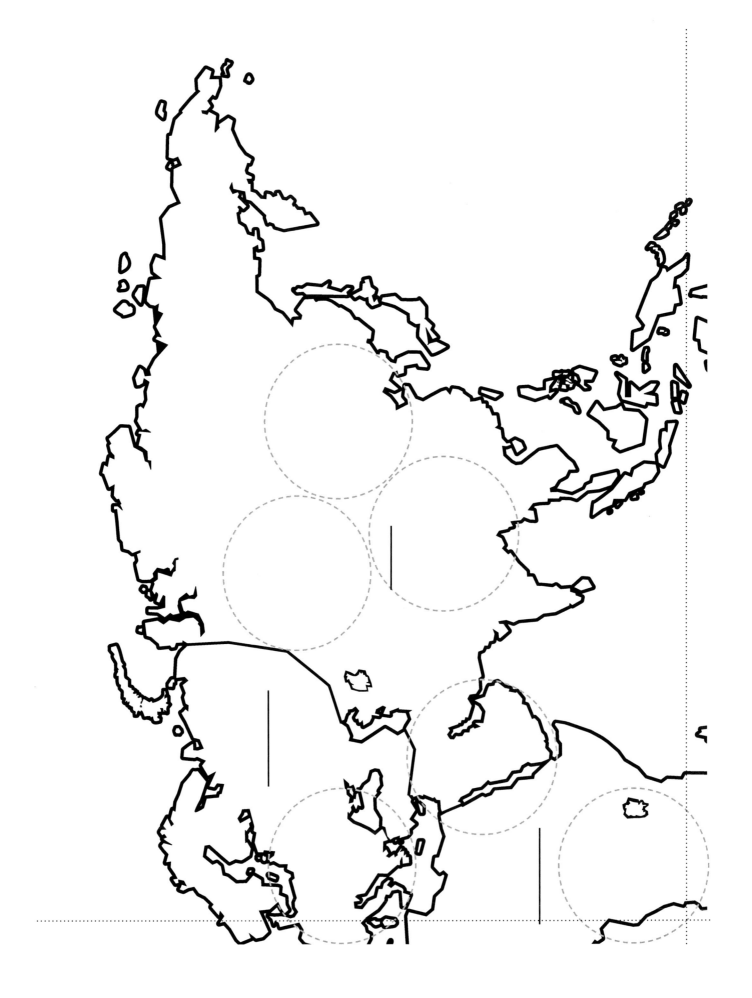

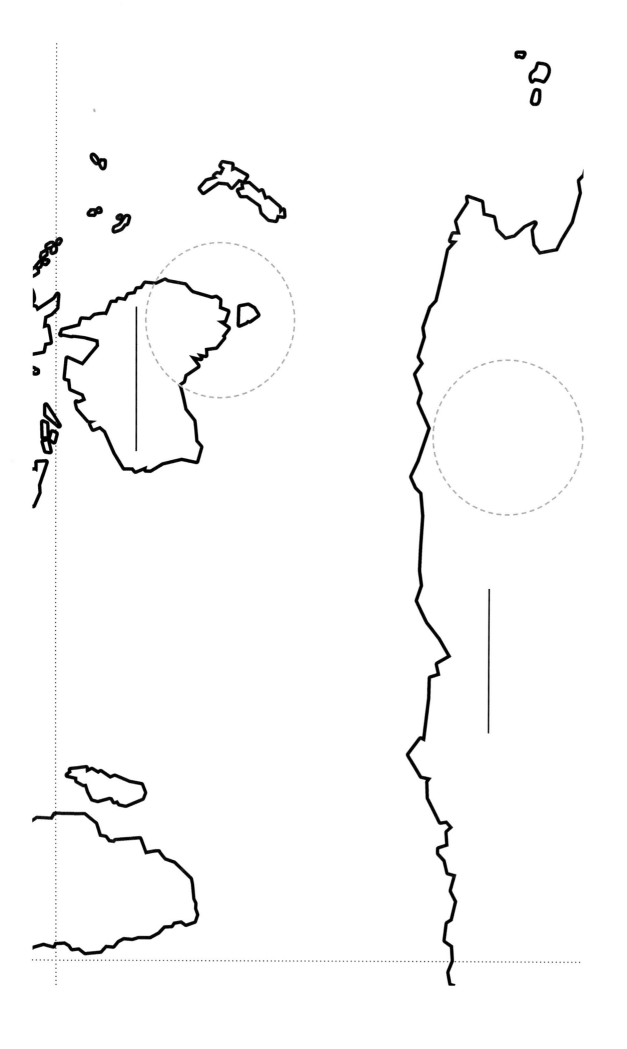

"In the land part of maps you will come across other real things like Mountains, Valleys, Hills, and Rivers. Mountains are very high parts of the land, and Valleys are very low parts," instructed Mr. Longitude.

"Hills are small mountains, and Rivers are like roads of water cutting through the land."

Cut out the four squares at the bottom of this page along the dotted lines and paste them on the square above that describes the picture the best.

a very high part of the land	a rounded higher part of land that is lower than a mountain
a very large natural stream of water	a very low part of the land

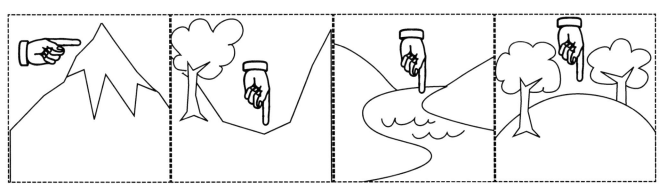

Below are pictures of things in our world like the mountains, rivers and hills that were not talked about in the story. Read the descriptions and draw lines from the picture to the description which best describes it.

LAKE:
a big amount of
water that has land
all around it

DESERT:
a very dry land
that has little rain
and few plants

ISLAND:
land that
has water all
around it

ICEBERG:
a big floating
piece of ice

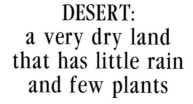

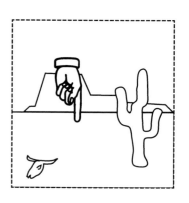

"On road maps there are often big or famous things called landmarks. Little symbols mark these on a map to help direct us around," added Mr. Longitude.

In addition to big and famous things, different places across the country are known for certain characteristics. On the map above, draw: sunglasses on Florida; a car on Michigan; a cowboy hat on Texas.; a rain cloud on Washington; a movie camera or TV on California; a potato on Idaho.

On the following pages are maps of the United States. Find your state, cut it out, glue it on another sheet of paper and draw landmarks on it or around it with arrows pointing to where those landmarks are.

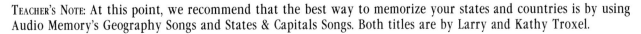

TEACHER'S NOTE: At this point, we recommend that the best way to memorize your states and countries is by using Audio Memory's Geography Songs and States & Capitals Songs. Both titles are by Larry and Kathy Troxel.

LEGENDS & LEAGUES

ALASKA

MARYLAND

ALABAMA

RHODE ISLAND

ARKANSAS

LOUISIANA

MICHIGAN

LEGENDS & LEAGUES

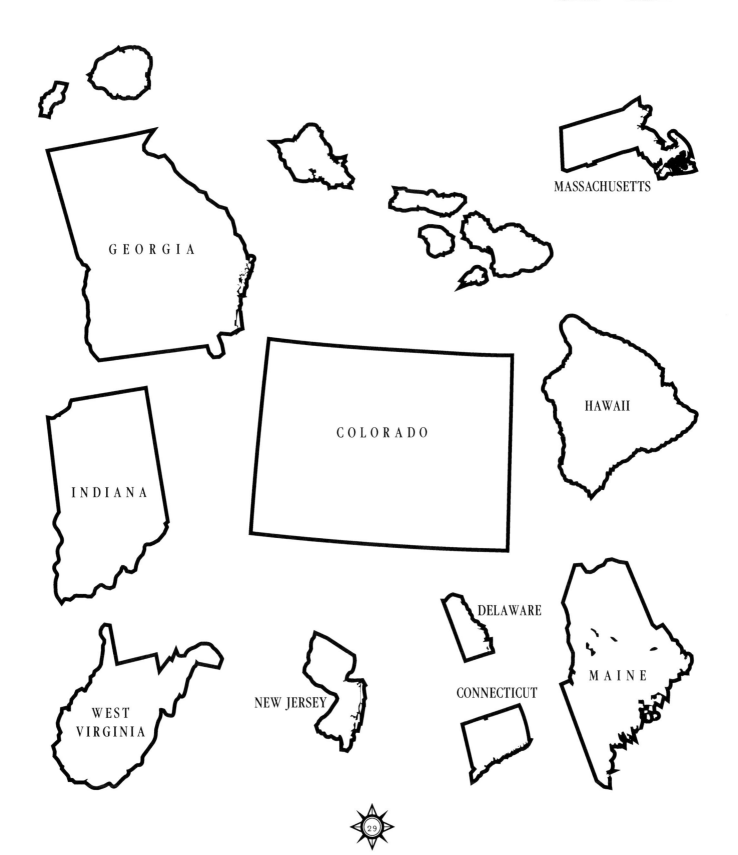

GEORGIA

MASSACHUSETTS

HAWAII

COLORADO

INDIANA

DELAWARE

MAINE

WEST
VIRGINIA

NEW JERSEY

CONNECTICUT

LEGENDS & LEAGUES

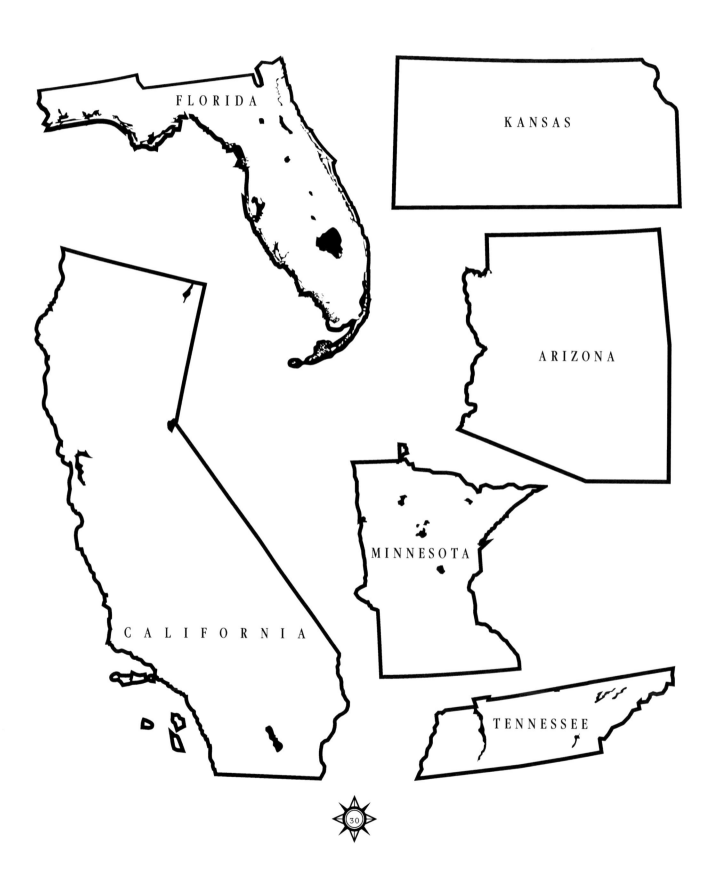

FLORIDA

KANSAS

ARIZONA

CALIFORNIA

MINNESOTA

TENNESSEE

LEGENDS & LEAGUES

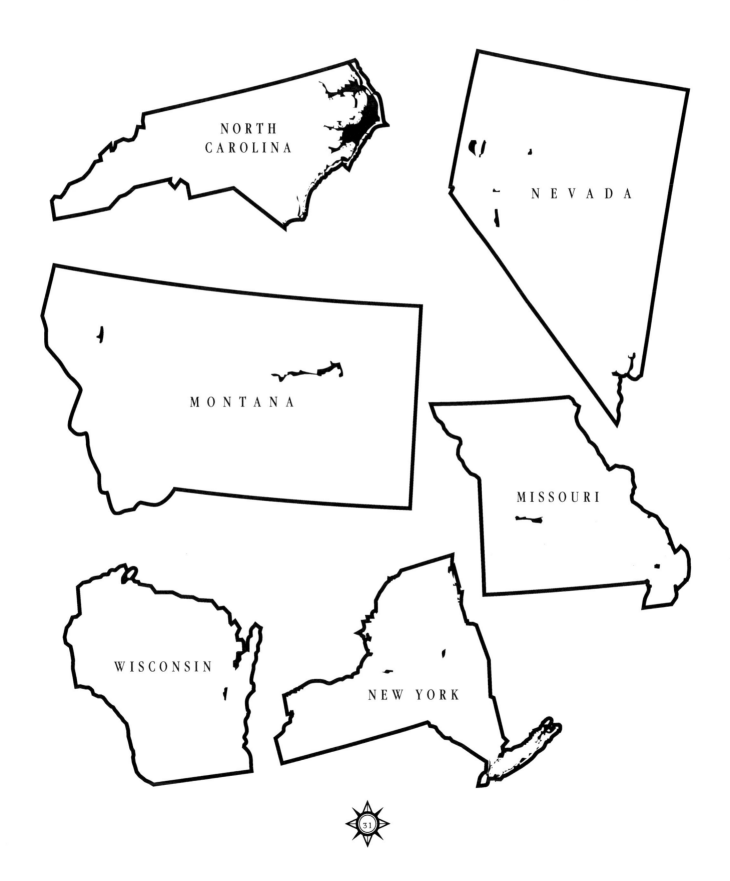

NORTH CAROLINA

NEVADA

MONTANA

MISSOURI

WISCONSIN

NEW YORK

LEGENDS & LEAGUES

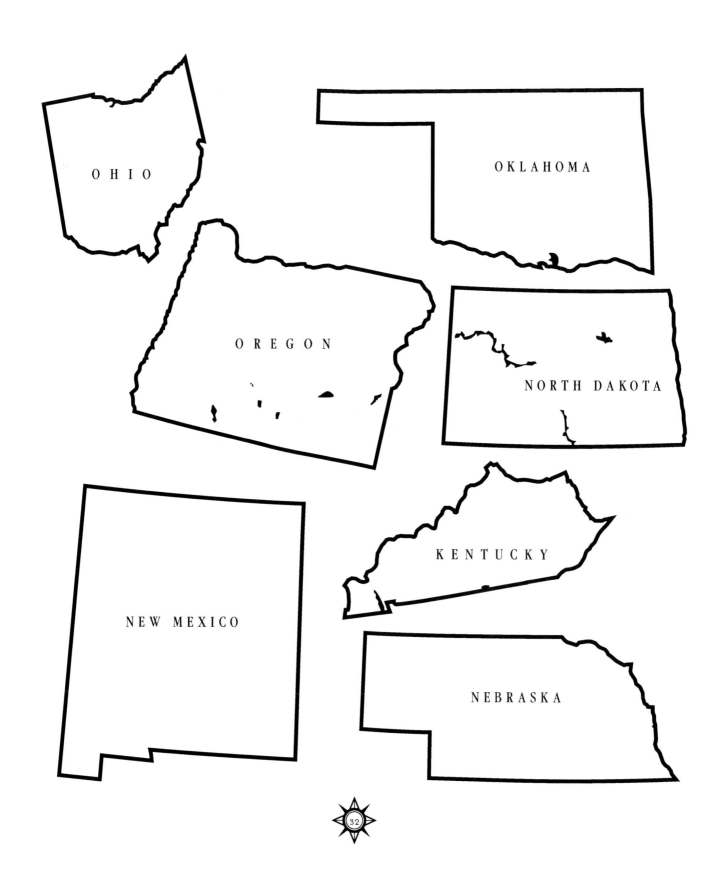

OHIO

OKLAHOMA

OREGON

NORTH DAKOTA

NEW MEXICO

KENTUCKY

NEBRASKA

LEGENDS & LEAGUES

IOWA

NEW HAMPSHIRE

ILLINOIS

MISSISSIPPI

SOUTH DAKOTA

VIRGINIA

UTAH

PENNSYLVANIA

SOUTH CAROLINA

LEGENDS & LEAGUES

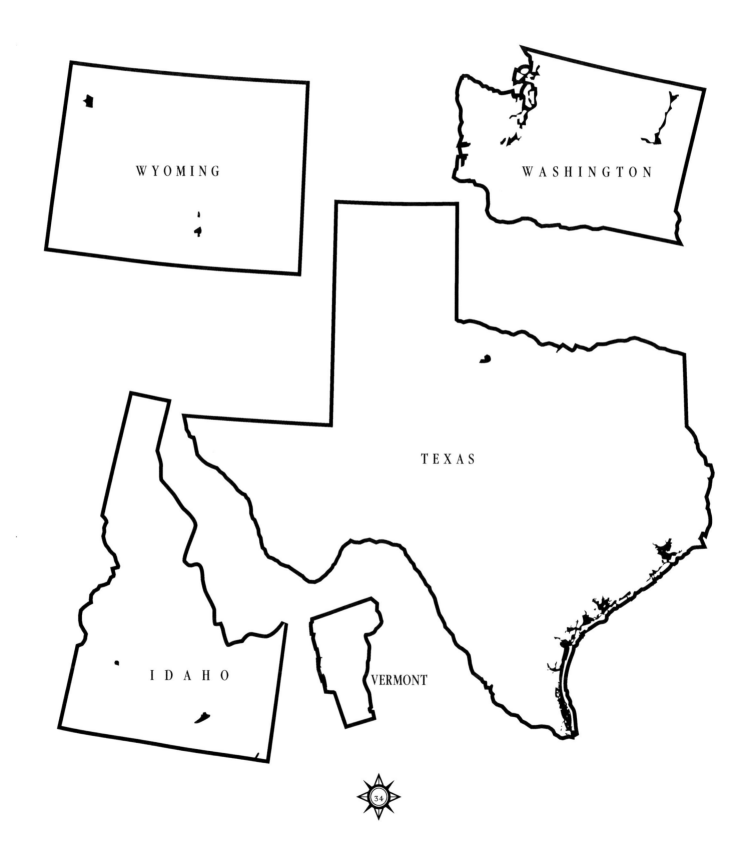

WYOMING

WASHINGTON

TEXAS

IDAHO

VERMONT

34

Color
MAGELLAN
PAGE 29

"Yet the world we live on is actually round like a ball. It is called a globe. And a man named Ferdinand Magellan proved this back in the year 1519 when he sailed all the way around it."

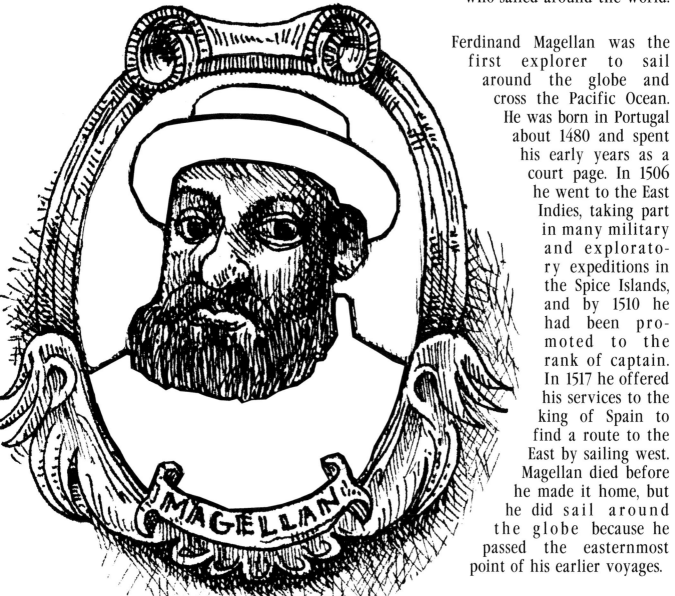

Color this picture of the first man who sailed around the world.

Ferdinand Magellan was the first explorer to sail around the globe and cross the Pacific Ocean. He was born in Portugal about 1480 and spent his early years as a court page. In 1506 he went to the East Indies, taking part in many military and exploratory expeditions in the Spice Islands, and by 1510 he had been promoted to the rank of captain. In 1517 he offered his services to the king of Spain to find a route to the East by sailing west. Magellan died before he made it home, but he did sail around the globe because he passed the easternmost point of his earlier voyages.

"Our round world is so big that when it is lunch time here, it is the middle of the night on the other side.

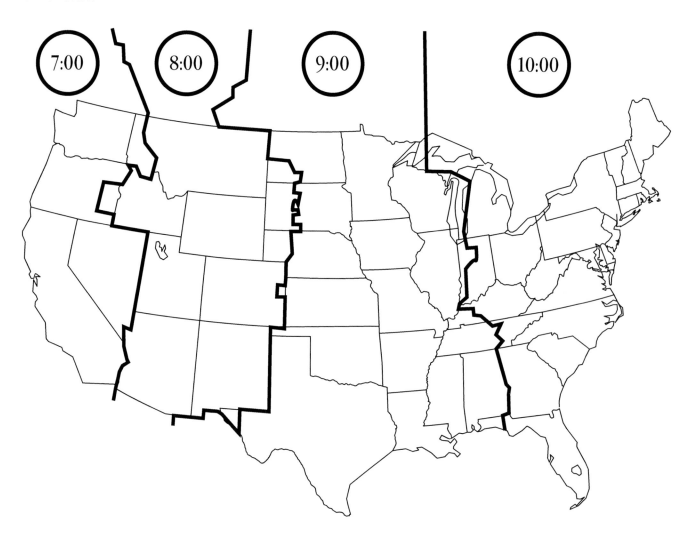

What time is it? The world is so big that it is different times at different locations—even within the same country. On the map above, the times are shown for four cities: Los Angeles, Denver, Chicago and Philadelphia. The heavy dark lines that snake down through the states divide the country into time zones. The time zones are called, from left to right: Pacific, Mountain, Central and Eastern. Color the time zone where you live in yellow.

LEGENDS & LEAGUES

"... we are not on the inside of the globe but walking on the outside of it. Yet in spite of the world being a globe, many of our most useful maps are flat."

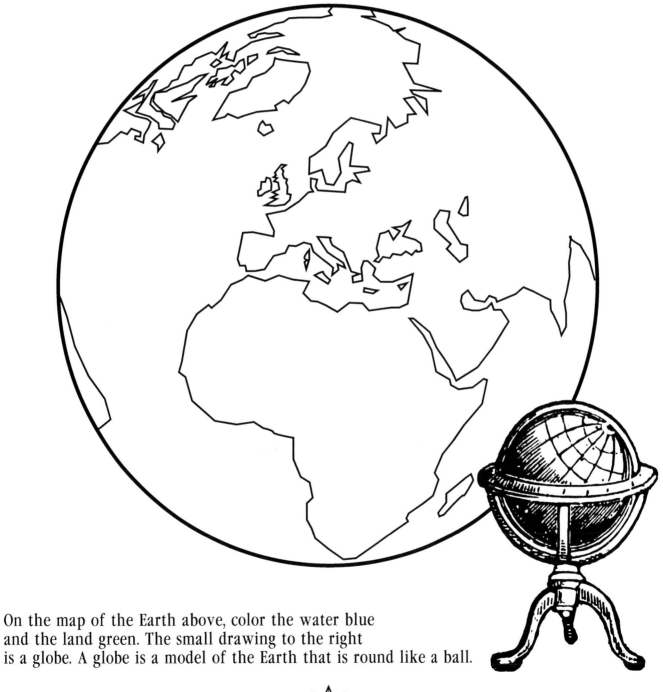

On the map of the Earth above, color the water blue
and the land green. The small drawing to the right
is a globe. A globe is a model of the Earth that is round like a ball.

"Maps can tell you how high places are and how far away one thing is from the other. Some maps will tell you how many steps to take . . ."

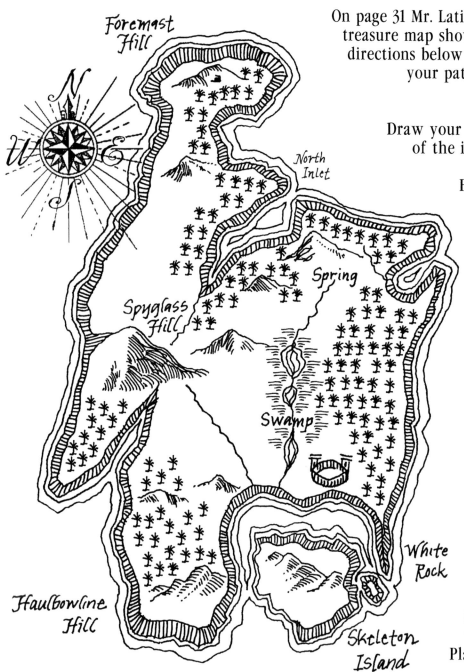

On page 31 Mr. Latitude is carrying the famous treasure map shown on this page. Follow the directions below using a dotted line to trace your path and place an X on where the treasure is buried.

Draw your boat anchored at the north of the island, east of Foremast Hill.

From the mouth of the cave in Foremast Hill go south.

Go to the east of the hill directly south of Foremast Hill and follow the coast to the southernmost point of North Inlet.

Proceed east to the Spring (it is a long, hot walk).

Follow the stream south, staying to the east of the Swamp.

Draw a straight line from the south tip of Skeleton Island to the north tip of the inlet that is directly south of Spyglass Hill.

At the fort north of Skeleton Island, turn to the west and cross the streams. Place an X on the line you've just drawn. Start digging!

"Some maps can tell . . . how many feet apart places are, and many tell you how many miles separate one spot from the other."

Determine the length and width of your classroom (or bedroom) by walking from one side to the other, putting one foot immediately in front of the other. Write down the number of steps it took to cross the room. Then have the teacher do the same thing and record the number of steps. Use one set of numbers and write them on the bottom of your map from page 8 with the explanation of to whose scale the map is drawn.

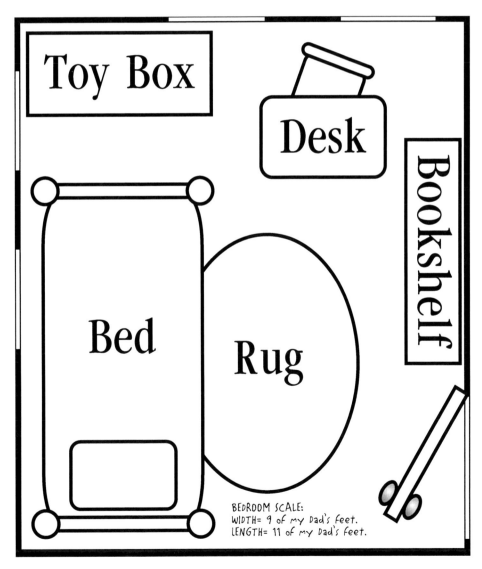

Toy Box

Desk

Bookshelf

Bed

Rug

BEDROOM SCALE:
WIDTH= 9 of my Dad's feet.
LENGTH= 11 of my Dad's feet.

LEGENDS & LEAGUES

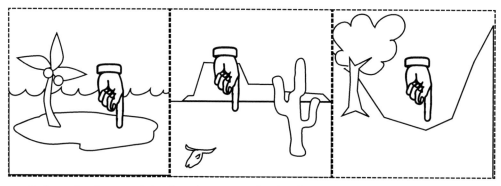

Color the box with the desert red, the box with the island blue,
and the box with the valley green.

Color the box with the animal who lives
at the North Pole red, and the animal
who lives at the South Pole blue.

Color the bird directly south of
the toucan red. Color the bird
directly north of the duck blue.
Color the bird directly east of
the eagle orange.

Circle the symbol for the airport, and draw
a box around the symbol for a hospital.

Final
EXAM

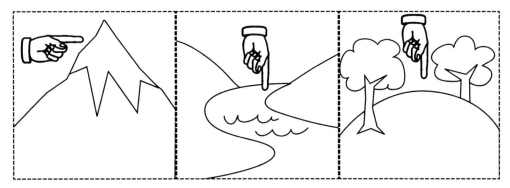

Write an H on the hill, an M on the mountain and an R on the river.

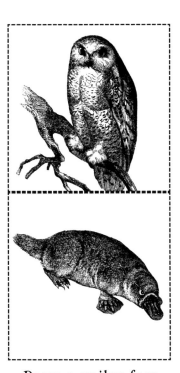

Draw a smiley face
on the box of the
animal that lives on
a continent in the
Southern Hemisphere

Color the land green.

Sing along with us as we row, row, row around the world and through geography.

Row, row, row your boat all a - round the map
North, South, East and West, round the com - pass goes; the
South is down be - low, North is on the top; the
Longitude is up and down Lati - tude left and right

Lat - i - tude and Long - i - tude, how much fun is that?
nee - dle's al - ways point - ing North where cold breez - es blow.
sun it ris - es in the East, West is where it drops.
lines lines on the map what a pret - ty sight!

LEGENDS & LEAGUES

Sing some more!

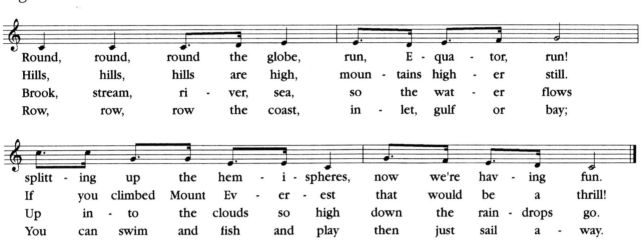

Round,	round,	round	the	globe,	run,	E -	qua	-	tor,	run!
Hills,	hills,	hills	are	high,	moun -	tains	high	-	er	still.
Brook,	stream,	ri -	ver,	sea,	so	the	wat	-	er	flows
Row,	row,	row	the	coast,	in -	let,	gulf	or	bay;

splitt	-	ing	up	the	hem	-	i	-	spheres,	now	we're	hav	-	ing	fun.
If	you	climbed	Mount	Ev	-	er	-	est	that	would	be	a	thrill!
Up	in	-	to	the	clouds	so	high	down	the	rain -	drops	go.
You	can	swim	and	fish	and	play	then	just	sail	a	-	way.

LEGENDS & LEAGUES

Following is a list of many geographical terms, some of which were introduced in *Legends & Leagues*. This resource is here to serve as an aid to the teacher to help explain geographical concepts should a question arise during the use of this program.

Bay: an inlet of the sea usually smaller than a gulf

Beach: sandy land along the edge of a lake or ocean

Brook: running water that flows into another body of water and is smaller than a creek

Canyon: a narrow valley that has high and steep slopes

Cape: a narrow piece of land that juts into the ocean

Cave: a deep hole under the ground

Channel: a narrow length of water

Coast: land that is by the ocean

Compass: a small device used to find north, south, east and west by using a magnetic needle, or the cross-shaped symbol drawn on maps to do the same thing

Continent: one of the seven biggest pieces of land in the world

Country: an invisible part of a continent claimed by a political state or nation

Creek: running water that flows into another body of water that is larger than a brook and smaller than a river

Desert: a hot land that gets very little rain

East: the direction in which the Sun comes up in the morning

Equator: a big imaginary circle on the earth that is equally distant from the North and South Poles, dividing the earth into the Northern and Southern Hemispheres

Globe: a round map of the earth

Gulf: an inlet of the sea usually bigger than a bay

Hill: a pile of land that is lower than a mountain

Iceberg: a very big block of floating ice

Island: land entirely surrounded by water

Isthmus: a narrow bit of land connecting two larger areas of land

Latitude: imaginary lines on a map that run around the world from East to West

Lake: a big, inland body of water

Longitude: imaginary lines on a map that run around the world from North to South

Map: something to look at to know how to get places that has big things drawn in small, simple pictures

Meridian: (see longitude)

Mountain: a big pile of land that is higher than a hill

North: the direction of the North Pole

North Pole: the top of the earth

Northern Hemisphere: the half of the earth that is above the equator

Ocean: the four largest bodies of water

Parallel: (see latitude)

Peninsula: a bit of land mostly surrounded by water

Plain: a large area of ground that is mostly flat

Pond: a body of still water that is smaller than a lake and bigger than a puddle

Province: a body of people living in a certain area in a country

River: a large body of running water that flows into another body of water

Road: an open way for people and cars to travel on

Scale: The difference between the big, real place and its size on a map

South: the direction of the South Pole

South Pole: the bottom of the earth

Southern Hemisphere: the half of the earth that is below the equator

State: a body of people living in a certain area in a country

Territory: an administrative subdivision of a country

Valley: a very low part of land, usually between hills or mountains

Volcano: a mountain that was made from hot melted rock

Waterfall: a river or creek that falls down from a higher ledge

West: the direction in which the Sun sets in the evening